Jar Projects

Presented
in honor
of
NORMAJEAN GRAYBILL
The Book Cellar
Valued Volunteer
2015

Jar Projects

Alice Vinten

NEW HOLLAND

First published in 2015 by New Holland Publishers Pty Ltd
London • Sydney • Auckland

The Chandlery Unit 009 50 Westminster Bridge Road
London SE1 7QY United Kingdom
1/66 Gibbes Street Chatswood NSW 2067 Australia
5/39 Woodside Ave Northcote, Auckland 0627

www.newhollandpublishers.com

A record of this book is held at the British Library and the
National Library of Australia.

ISBN 9781742576930

Managing Director: Fiona Schultz
Publisher: Diane Ward
Editor: Holly Willsher
Designer: Andrew Davies
Production Director: Olga Dementiev
Printer: Toppan Leefung Printing Limited
10 9 8 7 6 5 4 3 2 1

Keep up with New Holland Publishers on Facebook
www.facebook.com/NewHollandPublishers

Contents

Introduction

What is it about glass jars that makes them so difficult to throw away? While writing this book I have spoken to many people who have all confessed to having a few jars put by, waiting for a new lease of life, because they just couldn't bear to chuck them out. They're not sure why they do it either. I've always felt a temptation to hold on to them, way before the idea for this book had even started to grow in my mind.

I've been giving homemade gifts to my friends and family for years, so I've always found glass jars to be extremely useful. I'm a passionate upcycler, crafter and writer. I love to try pretty much anything that uses my hands, gives me a chance to be creative and express myself. I've written this book to share with you, not only the wonderful possibilities of upcycled projects, but also the pure joy of making things for other people and yourself.

If you are new to upcycling, then this book is the perfect way to get started. Glass jars are easily collected, reusable for lots of different purposes, and there are many small projects in this book that are suitable for beginners to try. You don't have to be particularly crafty to get started on these makes, as most of them have step-by-step instructions and guidance to talk you through each stage of making. Why not just give it a go? If, on the other hand, you're a dedicated crafter, then dive straight in and start modifying my designs to suit your own tastes. Each make in this book offers you plenty of opportunities to add your own little touches.

NOTE: I have referred to 'strong glue' throughout this book. The type of glue I am referring to is a multi-purpose, adjustable contact adhesive. It should be non-drip and high strength, suitable for most surfaces (especially non-porous ones such as glass) and allow time for you to adjust for exact positioning. You will find further details in the suppliers' section at the end of the book. Strong glue is usually thick and smelly, and you will probably need to apply a layer of it to both surfaces to be joined, allowing a few minutes for it to dry, before pressing your surfaces together. It is not washable, but it is waterproof and soap resistant so do be careful when you use it. However, compared to superglue, it is much more forgiving and pliable. Some (ok, I) have even said that it is quite therapeutic to peel the layers of glue from your fingers on an evening after a day's crafting!

Crafting and Upcycling

Craft is fun, creative and productive, and undoubtedly it can improve your health. Seriously, those who have hobbies, such as crafts, have improved levels of well being. Crafters have acknowledged this for a long time, but now health professionals are getting on board too. Occupational therapists use mind-stimulating hobbies, such as knitting and crochet, to alleviate the symptoms of depression. Craft hobbies are even thought to benefit the sufferers of Parkinson's disease by improving motor function.

Engaging in activities such as art, craft, and even home repair, can reduce the effects of stress-related conditions and even slow cognitive decline. Scientists say that this is because these types of activities stimulate the areas of the brain that control visual information, language and memories. Hobbies help because they 'fire' the neural connections, almost

like physical exercise, but for the brain. This helps people to retain functions that might otherwise decline, as they age. That's another endorsement for whiling away the hours, happily absorbed in your project.

As well as being good for you, crafting is a sure way to save yourself some money. Not only can you create perfect decorative items for your home, you can also make them match your colour scheme, your tastes, and all at less cost than you can buy them in a store. Bespoke usually means expensive, but not if you're doing it yourself! It's a great way to get the whole family involved too. The children

who never sit still will amaze you when they remain at your side, all afternoon, helping you with a fun crafty project.

Crafting with your children is a great thing to do for so many reasons. Firstly, and most importantly, you are spending time just with them, entirely focused on what they are doing, listening to their ideas and watching them create. All children really want is our time, after all, and crafting together is the perfect way to give it. Your child will be learning about imagination and self-expression, as well as the power of symbolic communication. Children enjoy the power they have over creating what they want, choosing their own design and expressing their emotions through shapes, colours and, generally, quite a lot of mess. Letting your child be free to experiment, splatter, spread and splodge, will not only ensure that they have a great time, but will also improve their confidence. If you are working with children, try not to be overbearing with design, symmetry and the overall 'look' of your projects. The end product is simply a result of the wonderful time your child has had crafting with you, and it most certainly doesn't have to be perfect. Coming from an obsessive perfectionist (when it comes to craft that is, housework; not so much) I know how hard this can be!

Experimenting with lots of different crafts, your child will also begin to develop their own preferences and interests. If they particularly like cutting and sticking, then maybe they can move on to making collages, for example. They can look back and feel proud of their makes and achievements; it's also useful for them to see how much they have improved over time. Why not try creating a little craft corner together? This will encourage them to begin creating independently.

While there are endless benefits of crafting with children, I think we all appreciate that a bit of crafting on our own is also just as precious. It gives us a welcome break from the pressures of daily life, helps the mind get into a calm and meditative-like state, and gives us that all-important confidence boost too! There's nothing quite like admiring something beautiful that you've made all by yourself. Well, we can allow ourselves to be smug sometimes, can't we?

Start your children upcycling early. Save all your cardboard boxes, egg boxes, cardboard tubes and plastic bottles. The ability to look at something plain and imagine what it could be turned into is a

great exercise in creativity. You'll have plenty of free craft materials to get started and your kids will be amazed by what they can make from simple items. But it's not just the children who can upcycle, why not have a go yourself? Make sure you regularly pop into your local thrift shops, junk stores and reclamation yard for inspiration. There are plenty of online sites and Facebook pages that give specific advice, tutorials and ideas for upcycling projects. Just put 'upcycling images' in your online search bar and browse through all the wonderful ideas! It'll have your creative juices flowing in no time.

If bargains make you smile, then upcycling is definitely for you. Finding something great for a small amount of money is such a thrill, and finding something for nothing is even better, which is totally possible in these days of excessive waste. You'll often find me unashamedly rummaging through my neighbours' skips, harassing builders about any unwanted wooden pallets they may have, and dragging various bits and bobs home to my already bursting garage. Thrifting, scavenging, junking, or whatever you want to call it, is getting ever more popular in these times of tightening belts and rising bills. Re-purposing old furniture is a great way of decorating your home on a tight budget. The beauty of it is that you will end up with bespoke, well-made furniture that you love, for a fraction of the price tag of a new purchase. Old, solid wood furniture is often well made, and may certainly be much sturdier than modern flat-packed items. It only takes a little elbow grease, some sandpaper and paint to transform these tired items into beautiful works of art. Each item you re-purpose, or make yourself, will be a talking point for you and your guests, and it's nice to show off your skills once in awhile too.

It's worth mentioning the considerable environmental benefits of upcycling. By upcycling an item instead of buying a new one, you'll be making a small difference to the grand scheme of things, and it's these small differences that really count. Each item you upcycle is an item that doesn't get thrown into landfill. It's also good to breathe new life into something that was once created by someone who cared about it.

Preparing, Decorating and Labelling Jam Jars

The first stage of making any of the projects in this book is to prepare your jars. Empty jars need to be cleaned. I usually put them through a hot cycle in the dishwasher. Sometimes this has the added bonus of removing the label, though if the label remains, I then soak the jars in a bowl of water. Soaking makes the paper soft, so that I can rub it off with my fingers. Once the paper label is off, you will probably be left with a sticky residue on the outside of your glass. There is a specific type of cleaning fluid that you can buy to remove this, or you can use white spirit. However, the 'sticky stuff remover' does smell less potent, and is kinder to your hands.

Ensure all of the gum has been removed from the jar before you start to work on it. If you are going to be using your jar to store edible items (such as those in the gifts chapter) then you will need to sterilise it before you begin. The dishwasher is usually hot enough to do this, or you could pop them into boiling water for half an hour or so. You could also place them on a baking sheet and bake them in the oven at 180°C/350°F for 10–15 minutes. Make sure the jars are the right way up and are not touching each other. Once they are clean and dry, you will want to fill them as soon as possible. When packing a jar with food, always try and reduce the amount of air bubbles present. This will make the content last longer.

I have specifically designed all of these projects so that they are easy for you to 'tweak', to suit your own tastes. You can change the colours, labelling or decorative details to suit your own style, and I absolutely welcome your creativity in this regard! To think that you will be having a go at my makes is wonderful enough in itself, and to know that they are getting your creative juices flowing is the best reward of all.

There are many options to consider when personalising your makes. Most of the gifts look better with added labels, and these can be as simple or as detailed as you like. If you have nice handwriting, you may like to write your labels and stick them on using a glue stick. If, like me, handwriting is not your strength, then you may prefer to print your labels, or use stamps. My little stamp kit has lasted years and was not very expensive. It has become invaluable for many of my craft projects.

Another possibility when thinking about labels is designing and ordering them online. This is a more expensive option, but if you look at it from a 'price per label' standpoint, it really isn't that pricey. If you regularly make homemade gifts then a professional label can really give them that extra finish. It's a lovely idea to include your family name on the label, so that the recipient of your gift can remember where it came from. There are websites that allow you to design your own labels, with hundreds of designs and layouts to choose from, the option of adding any pictures you may have, or choosing from theirs. I had so much fun designing mine that it is definitely something I will do again!

There are plenty of possibilities for embellishing the internal and external appearance of your jars. You can use ribbon, Washi tape, yarn, lace, glitter, wool, pom-poms, and decoupage, to name a few. The only time to be mindful is if you are considering placing candles in the jar. If this is the decoration you choose, you will need to ensure that nothing flammable is *inside* the jar, or even *around the neck* of the jar. You can tie ribbon around your tea-light projects, but always make sure that it is below the neck of the jar, and on the outside.

Once your jar decoration is decided, you will need to think about the lid. If you are choosing to spray paint your lids, please be aware that you should do this in a well ventilated area (preferably outside) and away from children, as the fumes may be headache inducing! Make sure that you cover the whole area in newspaper, or peg up an old sheet around your project. The ideal method for spray painting is to hold the can 20–30 cm /8–12 in away from the lid and keep the can moving. Make sure you shake the can well before you begin, and keep doing so every now and then, throughout your project.

Spray paint is great, as it is quick and easy to apply, dries fast, and you can spray more than one item at the same time. Note that some lids will have date stamps on them. These stamps will show through spray paint, so make sure to remove them with

a little white spirit before you start. It's a nice idea to place labels on your lids, or to stencil patterns on top. The best way to create a stencil is to use thick paper, or thin card (card stock), draw the shape in the centre and cut it out using a craft knife. Apply a thin layer of glue stick around the edge of the shape. Stick

it into place on the lid and then spray the paint on lightly, to prevent drips. Once the paint is completely dry, soak the lid in water and rub off the stencil.

Washi tape or high tack paper tape is great for covering lids. Both are available in attractive patterns and colours and are quick and easy to apply. A piece of pretty material, gathered around the neck of the jar with yarn or ribbon is a simple alternative. You can also use brown packing paper, as I have in the Hot Chocolate Jar project. This gives a traditional look. If you are cutting a circle of paper or material to cover your lid, you should first draw around the lid so that you have its size marked on the paper. Add 5 cm/2 inches to each side and you should end up cutting out a circle that is much bigger than your lid. This will allow plenty of room to secure the material with yarn around the neck of the jar. If you are left with excess paper or material, you can trim neatly around the jar until it is even on all sides.

So, now that I've covered all points of preparation and decoration, it's time to get started. I hope you enjoy making these projects as much as I did!

Gifts

I absolutely love to receive handmade gifts. Not only has the person who made them put their time, effort and care into producing them, but they've also considered me as an individual, my likes and dislikes, and come up with a gift that they know I'll be crazy for. From tasty homemade treats to fun and colourful surprises, I really do delight in delving into homemade presents.

In this chapter, you will find a variety of gifts to choose from, all wonderfully simple to make and a pleasure to receive. There are a couple of gifts to suit the 'foodies' among us, sweets (candies) for sugar addicts and chocoholics, a creative gift for baby, a crafty gift for a creative friend, and a welcome hand-soother for a friend or colleague who works hard with their hands all day. I think the best thing about making a gift for a loved one or relative is that excitement you feel in the pit of your stomach when you give the gift. Will they like it? Well, with these gifts, you can be sure they will!

Please refer to the introduction for details about the preparation of your jars before making any of the edible gifts in this section. This will ensure that your jars are safe and ready to be used for food. Let's get making.

Peppermint Creams

These fabulously colourful sweet treats evoke childhood memories. They are so easy to make and are one of the first recipes that children learn. They're a perfect size to pop into a jar, and their rich colours look great on display through the shiny glass.

Simple and quick to create, you can knock up a batch of these in an afternoon, leave them to chill in the refrigerator overnight, and they'll be ready to go the next day. And, if the creams themselves aren't enough, I've added a layer of delicious chocolate too! I found that a rich, dark (bittersweet) chocolate works best, cutting through the sweetness of the sugary peppermint.

You will need

* 1 large (US extra large) egg white

* 425 g/15 oz icing (confectioners') sugar, plus extra for dusting

* 175 g/6¼ oz dark (bittersweet) chocolate

* A few drops of peppermint extract

1   Whisk the egg white and peppermint extract together in a bowl until frothy, but not stiff.

2   Sift in the icing sugar, then use a wooden spoon to stir the mixture until it is thick and stiff. If it is too dry, add a few drops of water. If it is too soft and sticky, add some more icing sugar.

3   Dust the work surface with icing sugar and tip the mixture out onto it. Knead it until it has a smooth, clay-like consistency. Have a sheet of greaseproof/baking paper ready.

4   Pull a small lump, the size of a grape, from the dough and roll it into a ball between the palms of your hands.

5   Press the ball lightly onto the paper and then use a fork to flatten it into a disk. If your hands or fork stick to the mixture, simply dust them with a little icing sugar.

6   Repeat steps 4 and 5 until all of the dough is used up; you should have about 18. Transfer them to a shelf in the refrigerator to harden, this usually takes 1–2 hours.

7   Break the chocolate into small chunks and place in a heatproof glass bowl. Set the bowl over a saucepan of simmering water, so that the water does not touch the base of the bowl. Allow the chocolate to melt, stirring at the end to ensure all of the lumps have dissolved. Remove the bowl from the heat.

8 Remove the peppermint creams from the refrigerator. One at a time dip each cream into the melted chocolate. You only want to cover half of the peppermint cream. Replace it on the paper and continue until all the creams are covered. Return the creams to the refrigerator until the chocolate sets.

The peppermint creams should last a few weeks in an airtight container in the refrigerator, or in a cool room. However, I usually make mine about a week before I intend to give them away.

Presentation

When I was thinking about the presentation of this gift, I decided that I wanted something to match the lovely green colour of the peppermint. I used card stock with a fun zig-zag pattern that reminded me of the old-fashioned paper bags that confectioners use for their penny sweets.

Nutty Fudgy Bites

Like the peppermint creams, these sweet treats are simple to make, and are sure to become a staple recipe for gifts and last-minute guests.

If you, or your intended recipient, are not a fan of nuts, then you can simply omit them from the recipe. Or, why not try adding some raisins instead? If you want a more structured look to your fudge, then you can pour the mixture into a mould *before* you add the nuts, spread it flat and then press the chopped nuts into the top layer. If you want added wow factor, why not add some edible gold dust, glitter or sugar decorations? This simple recipe can easily be adapted to suit your needs.

You will need

* 400 g/14 oz can of sweetened condensed milk

* 30 g/1 oz butter

* 400 g/14 oz dark (bittersweet) or milk chocolate (around 50 per cent cocoa solids)

* 100 g/3½ oz icing (confectioners') sugar

* 60 g/2 oz chopped nuts (I used walnuts)

* You will also need a 20 cm/8 in square, shallow cake tin (pan), lined with greaseproof/baking paper.

1   Place the condensed milk and butter into a saucepan and set over medium heat. Break up the chocolate and add it to the saucepan. Melt all the ingredients together until smooth. Remove the mixture from the heat.

2   Sift over the icing sugar. Stir or whisk until smooth. Add the nuts and give the mixture a final stir before pouring it into the prepared tin. Press the fudge mixture down into the corners gently with the back of a spoon, to eliminate any air bubbles.

3   Chill in the refrigerator for about 1 hour, until the mixture is set. Turn out of the tin and cut into little squares. I like to keep the squares small. The fudge is so rich, just a mouthful will do!

Presentation

For my fudge jars I have used exactly the same design as for my peppermint creams, except I have substituted the green for red.

Cookies in a Jar — Baking Kit

When I first heard of this idea I couldn't decide why I hadn't thought of it! It's so simple and really takes all the weighing and measuring out of baking a batch of yummy oat cookies for the lucky recipient. It also looks very attractive when layered in the jar. You can accessorise your gift with colourful labels and tie on some added extras, such as cookie cutters, or a bag of cookie decorations, if you like.

For this recipe you will need a 1 litre (1 3/4 pint) jar. When packing the jar, it's important to push each layer firmly down so that you can fit it all in.

You will need

* 115 g/4 oz plain (all purpose) flour
* 1 teaspoon baking soda
* ½ teaspoon salt
* 1 teaspoon ground cinnamon
* ¼ teaspoon ground nutmeg
* 100 g/3 1/2 oz granulated (white) sugar
* 100 g/3 1/2 oz brown sugar
* 175 g/6 oz rolled oats
* 150 g/5 oz raisins

1 In a small bowl, mix the flour with the sugar, baking soda, salt, cinnamon and nutmeg. This mixture will form the white layers in the jar.

2 Pour half of the flour mixture into the jar. Add the brown sugar in an even layer. Top this with the rest of the flour mixture. Tip the rolled oats in next, followed by the raisins.

3 Press down the ingredients firmly and close the lid tightly.

4 I typed my baking instructions on my home computer in a fairly small type size and then printed them out. I popped them underneath the coloured paper, which I have used to cover the lid of the jar. This way they are tucked out of sight until ready to be used.

Another option is to cut out a rectangle of thin card, fold it in half and make a tag that has the making and baking instructions written on it. Punch a hole through one corner of the tag and attach it to the jar using ribbon or twine.

Neatly write or print a recipe card with the following instructions:

Oaty Raisin Cookies Kit

Method
Pre-heat the oven to 180°C/350°F/Gas mark 4.

1 Empty the contents of the jar into a large bowl and stir until well mixed.

2 Add 175 g/6 oz softened butter, 1 egg and 1 teaspoon vanilla extract and mix together thoroughly.

3 Spoon heaped teaspoons of dough onto a baking sheet lined with greaseproof/baking paper, leaving enough space between for the cookies to spread.

4 Bake for 10 minutes, or until the edges are lightly brown. Allow to cool and set for 5–10 minutes before transferring to a wire rack to cool.

Presentation

1 I used brightly patterned paper to cover the lid of my jar. I wanted something bright and funky to match the colourful cookie cutters that I intended on adding to the gift. Cut out a large circle of paper, roughly 5 cm/2 in wider than the diameter of the lid. Place it on top of the lid and press it down around the sides.

2 Take some string, yarn or ribbon, and thread on your label and cookie cutters. Tie the yarn around the lid and tighten it gently as you push it down over the paper onto the neck of the jar. This bit can be slightly tricky. Tie a yarn bow tightly. If your paper is not sitting flat on the top of the jar, simply pull the edges downward until it flattens out. You will have excess paper at this stage, and can now cut neatly around the circle so that your edges are tidy.

3 All that's left is to add a cute label, cut to any size and shape (I've chosen a heart!) and your gift is ready for a lucky friend or relative. I always use a water-based glue stick to attach my labels, which is easy to wash off when the jar is (hopefully) re-used!

Hot Chocolate Jar

This is, by far, one of the easiest makes in the whole book, if you know a chocolate lover, then you have the ideal person to make this gift for. Not only is it easy and quick to make, but it's pretty and practical too. The layers of fluffy pink marshmallow rest perfectly beside the light and dark chocolate chips. A lovely touch would be to add a small whisk to this gift, by threading it onto the ribbon at the top. Make sure that it is shorter than the height of your jar though, or it becomes tricky to present nicely.

You will need

* Brown paper

* Ribbon of your choice

* Small whisk

* Mini marshmallows

* Chocolate chips

* Coloured card (card stock)

1 Choose a suitable jar. Make sure it is clean and thoroughly sterilised.

2 Take a handful of chocolate chips and layer them across the base of the jar, followed by a layer of mini marshmallows. Repeat the layers until your jar is full.

Presentation

As the marshmallows are so colourful, I've chosen plain brown paper to cover the lid of my jar. I've used brown string to hold the paper in place and to attach a whisk and label. You can either use the words that I have suggested (to the right), or write your own version, on the label.

Hot Chocolate Jar

Method

Take a microwave-safe mug and fill it with milk. Pop in a handful of chocolate chips and heat for 30 seconds on high. Remove and whisk. Place the mug back into the microwave, heat for another 30 seconds, then remove and whisk until rich and frothy. Scatter on a liberal handful of mini marshmallows and carefully carry to the nearest sofa. Enjoy.

A Hot Chocolate Jar can be made up way in advance (check your chocolate chip and marshmallow labels for storage times) and kept for a time when you need that emergency gift. Just store it in a cool place.

Sewing Kit

I simply love the idea of this make. It appeals to both the crafter and the avid up-cycler in me – the best of both worlds! We've all needed a sewing kit at some point, and this is such an appealing one to present to a crafty friend. You could even adapt the kit to include a small sewing project. It's really up to you what you put into your sewing kit. Think about the person you are making it for, and adapt it to suit their tastes.

These mini sewing kits are growing in popularity and I've seen many online and in crafting magazines, so I have tried to make mine a little different. Instead of the traditional pin cushion topper made from fabric and stuffing, I have used brightly coloured, miniature pom-poms.

You will need

* Spray paint

* Strong glue

* Mini pom-poms in various sizes and colours

* Sewing accessories of your choice, such as: pack of needles, reel of thread, thimble, small scissors, measuring tape, selections of buttons, length of sequins, length of ribbon and two safety pins.

1 Choose the pom-poms that you are going to use on the lid. You will need 5 or 6 larger pom-poms, each 2.5 cm/1 in diameter and a mix of smaller sizes. Most packs will provide plenty to choose from in sizes and colours.

2 Depending on the colour of your pom-poms, decide what colour you are going to paint the lid, so that the colour complements your scheme. Cover any work surfaces with newspaper, then spray the lid in a well ventilated area. Leave to dry.

3 Apply a thick layer of glue to the top of the lid, and stick three of the large pom-poms in the centre. Use the ones you like least because they are less likely to be visible.

4 Now use a mixture of smaller pom-poms and stick them all around the larger ones, to cover the lid.

5 Build up the layers using glue, until you have a rough dome shape and the first pom-poms are covered. Set aside to dry completely.

Presentation

Fill your jar. I haven't added any labels to this make as I think it is self-explanatory.

Hand Scrub

This jar makes a great gift for anyone who works with their hands. The main ingredient (apart from the sugar) in this recipe is the coconut oil. You should look to buy 'cosmetic grade' coconut oil, which is readily available online. At room temperature it is a white solid, with a similar texture to butter. For this scrub, you will need your coconut oil to be solid but softened.

This recipe provides you with a coarse, exfoliating scrub. If you would like a scrub with less 'aargh' and more 'ahhhh' then simply adjust the ratio of coconut oil to sugar; use less sugar and more coconut oil. This scrub will have a shorter shelf life than store bought scrubs, as it is made with all natural, perishable ingredients. Small jars work well for this gift, as your recipient will want to use it up within about a month or so. I've used a small jar for my scrub.

You will need

* Coconut oil, softened

* Granulated (white) sugar

* 1 lemon

* Lavender essential oil

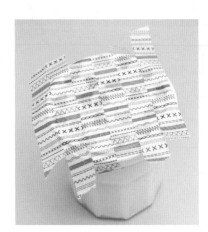

1   Choose the jar that you'd like to store your scrub in and make sure it is clean and sterilised. Fill it to just under halfway with sugar. Tip the sugar into a mixing bowl.

2   Spoon coconut oil into the jar until you have about the same quantity as the sugar, and then add it to the bowl.

3   Add the juice of half a lemon and about 5 or 6 drops of lavender oil to the bowl. Using your hands, mix it all together until everything is well combined.

4   If you'd like to add a little colour to your scrub then why not try adding some zest from the lemon for a pretty yellow tint.

Note that some essential oils may provoke allergic reactions. **All essential oils should be avoided by women in the first trimester of their pregnancy.** Also, some oils can make the skin more sensitive to sunlight, so please ensure you read any labelling when purchasing essential oils. That said, the recipe I provide for this project uses lavender oil, considered a 'safe' essential oil with very low allergen levels.

Presentation

1   I have decorated the lid of my jar with washi tape. It's so easy to apply to a lid and you can tuck it under the rim nicely so that it doesn't interfere with opening and closing the jar. I have also used a white label, decorated with my stamp set and some yarn and a bow to really set off the design.

To use, simply scoop a dollop between your fingers, rub in vigorously and then rinse with water. You will find that you are left with a slippery residue of coconut oil; simply pat your hands dry and rub the remaining oil into your skin. It will leave your hands feeling silky and smooth. It's great for elbows too!

Spice Mix

In a rare, quiet moment in the kitchen I found myself picking up a much used spice bottle and reading the ingredients. Displaying itself as 'cajun', it seemed to contain nothing of the real flavours of Cajun cooking. Instead, I found myself looking at strange chemical sounding words. This was the perfect motivation to create my own spice mixes!

It is best to make up spice mixes in relatively small amounts. I find that baby food jars and small round jars are the best receptacles, they look sweet and you could even make a little set of two or three different varieties. For flavour that really packs a punch, you could try roasting whole spices in a hot pan before grinding them in a pestle and mortar. This works especially well if you are making spices for a curry.

I have provided two recipes that have proved to be popular.

BBQ Meat Rub

The components of this mix can be layered into a jar and then shaken before needed. Doing it this way means that it not only tastes great, but will look pretty. It is best rubbed directly onto meat and poultry before grilling or barbequing.

* 6 tablespoons coconut sugar

* 1 tablespoon chilli powder

* ½ teaspoon coarse black pepper

* ½ teaspoon cayenne pepper

* ½ teaspoon dried thyme

* ½ teaspoon onion powder

* 1 teaspoon garlic salt

Curry Mix

This is a staple mix that I use in curries. I also use it to marinate the meat before I fry it with onions, add coconut milk and fresh or canned tomatoes. This also works without the coconut milk, for a lower fat option. The amounts below are for one family meal; to fill a jar with this mix, double or treble the amounts, ensuring that it is well mixed before use, and letting the recipient know how much to use.

* 1 tablespoon ground cumin

* 1 tablespoon ground coriander

* 1 tablespoon garam masala

* 2 teaspoons smoked paprika

* 1 teaspoon fenugreek powder

* ½ teaspoon turmeric

Presentation

These mixes are easy to dress up as gifts; a simple raffia bow and label are all you'll need.

Pom-Pom Baby Garland

I remember the time when making a pom-pom was like setting out on a small but challenging expedition, involving cardboard circles and sore wrists. Thankfully, modern technology has finally provided us with a super-quick, super-easy, plastic pom-pom maker. There's nothing quite like the smugness I feel after I've made pom after perfect pom on these wonderful contraptions. The Pom-Pom Baby Garland uses cute little pom-poms. You can choose how long you want the garland to be, the colours you'd like to use, and how far apart you'd like to string the pom-poms. I have chosen some really bright colours for my garland: I just can't help myself. However, these would look lovely in neutrals, pastels, or even black and white. Any jar will do for this gift, but a slightly larger one is best as it won't squash the pom-poms.

You will need

* Wool

* 1 wool needle

* 1 pom-pom maker (you can do it the traditional way, if you know how)

1 Make the pom-poms, following the instructions on the pom-pom maker. Around 16 small pom-poms (finished size 3.5 cm/1^{1}/4 in) should give you nearly 3 m (10 ft) of garland.

2 Trim the pom-poms with sharp scissors to cut off any longer strands.

3 Thread your wool needle with your chosen wool. Push the needle right into the centre of the pom-pom (where the knot is) and through to the other side. Continue to string the pom-poms onto the wool in this manner until you have used them all.

Presentation

1 I have used a label with a personal touch for the top of the jar.

2 A string of lace ribbon around the lid of the jar is my finishing touch.

Kids

Prepare to enter the world of crazy makes, shark attacks, felt vegetables and aliens. Yes, it's the children's projects. I've certainly enjoyed experimenting with my own children, who proved to be the inspiration for most of the makes in this chapter. I've learnt how they will play with something I've made them, or something we've made together, for much longer than a toy I've bought in a store. I've learnt how they love to show off the creative gifts, the ones that only they have, and display them on their shelves.

Welcome to the world of whimsy, magic and intrigue, I ask you to embrace joyfully the wonderful list of weird stuff that you can stick in jars.

A Jar of Kong

It's whacky, it's a bit random, it's definitely awesome, and my kids love it! It's a jar of Kong. There is no real 'why' to this make, so I'm not going to talk about the inspiration, mood or ethos of my design. I had a tall jar, a toy gorilla and a spice jar. So naturally, this is what I made.

You will need

* Glass or plastic spice pot (empty and clean, with a flat square lid)

* Silver spray paint

* Small plastic gorilla (or lizard)

* Glass jar

* Strong glue

* Glass paint pens

* Black permanent marker

1   The spice pot will become the skyscraper. In a well ventilated area protected with newspaper, spray the spice pot silver. Leave it to dry completely.

2   With the lid on the work surface, representing the base of the skycraper, use the marker pen to draw squares to represent windows, evenly around the spice jar. Use the glass pens to add some flames bursting out of the windows, if you wish. Leave to dry.

3   Once the paint has dried, apply strong glue to the spice jar lid and stick it to the inside of the jar lid. Allow to dry completely.

4   Turn the jar so that the base is at the top. Start to draw flames all the way round from the neck of the jar, part way up. Start with a yellow pen and draw long thin spikes starting from the neck of the jar, to look as if flames are climbing the walls of the skyscraper. Make them different heights to resemble real flames. Leave to dry, then repeat the process with the orange pen, and then the red pen.

5   Stick the gorilla to the 'top' of the skyscraper using strong glue and allow to dry.

6   To assemble, carefully push Kong and the skyscraper into the jar and secure the lid.

Presentation

I have sprayed the lid and top of the jar silver, to give it a more industrial feel. I have also added a warning sign to the lid, using striped black and white paper and my stamp set.

Fairy Grotto

Fairies – check! Flying white horse – Check! Pink flowers – Check! Fairy Lights – Oh yes.

   The fairy lights that I have used are a string of ten, with LED bulbs and a battery pack. They are great for children's projects as they don't get hot and there's no risk of electrocution! Try to find a large jar with a wide neck for this make, it will make it easier when trying to get everything in later.

   I have sourced some great craft buttons with a 'fairy' theme for this project, but you can just as easily use pictures cut from an old book or magazine. I have snipped off the back of my buttons with wire cutters before sticking them on, so that they lie flat. This grotto looks so pretty when lit up, and would make a fabulous night-light for a little girl's (or boy's!) room.

You will need

* String of battery operated fairly lights

* Crepe paper, green and pink (or another other floral colour)

* Glue stick

* Strong glue

* Fairy-themed craft buttons

* Wide cardboard tube (kitchen roll size)

1   To make the fairy lights into a stem of flowers, cut a long 2.5 cm/1 in wide strip of green crepe paper. Apply glue stick to one side and then, starting at the battery pack, wrap the paper around the wire of the fairy lights. Continue to do this until all of the wire is covered.

2   To make each flower, cut a small rectangle of crepe paper 5 x 2.5 cm/2 x 1 in. Cut into the rectangle, feathering one long edge. These will be your petals.

3 Add glue stick to the edge opposite the petals and wrap the crepe paper around an LED bulb. Fold some of the petals back so that they look like flowers. Cover any visible wire with green crepe paper.

4 Cut the cardboard roll to the same length as the height of the jar, so that it will fit inside with the lid closed. The cardboard tube is used to hide the battery pack. Wrap the cardboard in green crepe paper and secure with glue stick. Slide the battery pack into the cardboard roll, to make sure it fits.

IMPORTANT: Remember that your battery pack on/off switch will need to be accessible when you open the jar. The on/off switch will be at the bottom of the design.

5 Keeping the battery pack inside the roll, start to wind the green stemmed wire around the tube, arranging the fairy light flowers in an attractive manner. To secure it, tuck the last fairy light under a wire somewhere, or use your glue stick.

6 Fill the tube with scrunched up crepe paper until the battery pack is sitting at the end that will fit inside the lid, but still hidden within the tube.

7 Stick on the fairy craft buttons and add glitter. Carefully push the fairy grotto into the jar.

Glowing Space Jar

I think that this is one of my son's favourite objects. It has been proudly displayed on the 'special stuff' shelf in his room ever since the glue dried, nestled alongside other important things. It is hard to portray in a photograph just how great this looks when it is glowing in the dark.

I used craft buttons in this project, this time with a space theme. If you wanted to use images cut out from magazines, or even draw your own and cut them out, then that would be fine too. My space buttons set included a rocket, two spaceships and two aliens.

Imagine your children's delight when you tell them that you have not only captured aliens, but a whole alien world, all inside a jar! Not only is this space jar super fun to gaze into, but it also makes an excellent night light, providing a gentle glow which fades by morning.

1 Cut a piece of wire, 20 cm/8 in long, and push one end of it into the polystyrene ball. Make sure that it is pushed in far enough so that your ball is secure.

IMPORTANT: The paint will ever so slightly melt the surface of the ball. The ball will have a slightly mottled and rock-like appearance – perfect for an alien planet! Set the wire into a jar or glass to allow the paint to dry completely. Tape some masking tape around the ball in a random pattern before spraying with another colour.

You will need

* Glow in the dark glass pens

* Aliens and spaceship buttons

* A polystyrene (styrofoam) ball

* Modelling wire and wire cutters

* Spray paint in bright neon colours **OR** water-based paint mixed with PVA glue

* Strong glue

* Masking tape

2 If you are using a water-based paint, mix it with some PVA glue (about half paint, half glue) so that it adheres to the polystyrene as you paint. Allow to dry then add some stripes in a different colour.

3 If you are using spray paint, hold the wire in one hand, with the ball at arms length in a well ventilated area (preferably outside). Spray it your chosen colour, using a light mist, and holding the can 20–30 cm/ 8–12 in away from the sphere.

4 The painted ball will become a 'planet' and needs fixing to the inside lid of the jar. Curl the end of the wire around into a circle and place it against a flat surface, while bending the rest of the wire to a 90 degree angle. The planet will appear as if suspended in mid air. Glue the wire circle to the inside jar lid. Allow to dry completely.

5 To prepare the aliens and spaceships, if you are using buttons, loop some wire through the buttonholes and fix into place with glue. You want the wire to stick down beneath your aliens, so that when you push it into your planet, they will look like they are standing on top of it. If you are using paper cut-outs or hand drawn aliens, simply tape a length of wire onto the back of each.

Alternatively, if you want your shapes to lie flat on the planet, snip off the loops on the buttons with your wire cutters, and use a glue stick to attach them.

6 If you have a rocket-shaped button, you may want to consider using a longer wire and have it 'flying' over the planet. Just remember to fix everything close enough to the ball that you can still fit it through the neck of the jar!

7 Once the glue is dry, fix the characters to the planet by pushing the wire straight into the polystyrene ball. If they are a little loose, glue the wire ends and pop them back into the hole you made.

Presentation

1 Paint a square on one side of the glass to act as a 'viewing window' for the aliens, using black glass paint. Paint glow-in-the-dark stars onto the outer glass jar around the viewing window. Simply apply a blob of yellow paint onto the glass, and then use the tip of the pen to drag the paint out in all different directions to make a star.

2 Use a different coloured glow pen and cover the rest of the glass in small dots. Allow to dry, and then apply a second coat to ensure that the stars will glow really brightly.

3 Spray paint the lid silver. Push the planet into the jar and secure the lid.

IMPORTANT: Do not use your strong glue directly on the polystyrene ball as it will melt it! Always use water-based glue and paint when working with polystyrene.

Toy lid 'Little Bits' Jars

If, like my kids, your little darlings like to pick up and save all manner of small, easy-to-lose items, then these small jars are ideal for you. Perfect for acorns, stones, miniature cars, small bouncy balls, tiny plastic weapons, hair clips, sequins and much, much more, these jars not only look good, but provide a valuable service.

Although your glue will hold the toys in place, they will weaken if constantly twisted, so remind your child to open the jars by twisting the lids, not the toys!

You will need

* Small plastic toys that are no longer played with

* Spray paint

* Strong glue

1 Choose a selection of jars in a suitable size.

2 Ask your children to choose some small-scale toys that are no longer favoured to fit the lids. Choose toys with a flat solid base, or feet that fit onto your jar lids.

3 Ensure that the lids are clean from grease or dust. Apply strong glue and fix the toys in place on top of the lids. Set aside to dry.

4 Spray paint the lids in a well ventilated area protected with newspaper. They may need several coats to get a smooth even colour, especially when using light colours such as yellow. Leave the paint to dry.

Glow Worms

This is a fun project that your kids will love. If you think that they're too cute to be kept in a jar, you could use them as decoration for a child's room, or a night-light. If you have slightly older children, around 7 and up, then they'll love to help you make these adorable glowing bugs.

This project is a little fiddly at points, but it's well worth persevering. The glow is provided by a string of battery-operated fairy lights. Choose a jar with plenty of room and a wide neck if possible. A jar of glow worms really does conjure up the image of a quintessential childhood, of summer afternoons spent foraging in woods and coming home exhausted, sporting grubby faces and grass-stained knees.

You will need

* A string of battery operated LED fairy lights

* Black, green, red, orange, and purple crepe paper

* Brown paper (optional)

* Orange soft cardboard (optional)

* Red pom-poms (roughly 1 cm/3/8 in diameter or larger)

* Googly eyes

* Glue stick

* Strong glue

* PVA glue

* 1 paintbrush

* Green garden wire

* Wire cutters

* Pen or pencil

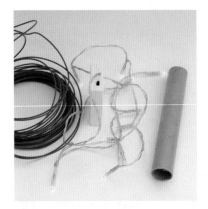

1 To make the shape of the glow worm bodies. Wrap a 10 cm/4 in length of green garden wire around a pen or pencil until you have 4 or 5 wraps. Leave a straight length of wire at the end.

2 Slide the wire off the pen and stretch it slightly so that it opens up a little, making it longer and wider. Place the coil over one of the bulbs on the fairy lights, and wrap the end of the wire around the plastic to secure it. Cut off any excess wire.

3 Cut the green crepe paper into ten strips each 2.5 cm/1 in wide and 10 cm/4 in long.

4 Prepare a little dish of PVA glue mixed with water (about ²⁄₃ PVA glue to ¹⁄₃ water) so that you have quite a thick consistency.

6 Paint the crepe paper with PVA glue mixture, gently brushing down all of the folds to form a smooth shape. This will be the worm's body. Repeat steps 1 to 5 for all of the bulbs. Hang them up to dry.

8 Meanwhile, cut out the leaf shapes from the rest of your crepe paper and brown paper. I have used mostly crepe paper, but found that a sheet of brown paper or soft card in every bunch of leaves gave the foliage a more pleasing shape and structure. Fold the paper into half before cutting the leaf shapes, this will allow you to get two leaves with each cut, and they are easier to fold over the wire if they are left joined at the bottom.

9 Wrap the rest of the exposed wire with black or brown crepe paper. Use a little glue applied to a long thin strip of paper, and wrap it around until you cover all of the exposed plastic.

5 Brush a strip of crepe paper lightly with glue and wrap it loosely around the wire coil. Make sure to cover all of the wire and to fold over the paper at the end so that it completely encloses the bulb within the paper.

7 Glue the red pom-poms to the green bodies, at the opposite end to the bulbs (which will be the glow worms glowing bottoms!). Stick them to the end closest to the wire. Set aside and allow to dry. Stick googly eyes to each pom-pom.

10 Group your leaves into threes or fours, including one sheet of brown paper or card in each group. Apply glue to the centre of the leaves and then fold over the wire. Once you have stuck on all of your leaves, fold them down the centre to give them a more leaf-like appearance.

11 If you want to keep your worms in the jar permanently then follow the next few steps. However, if you want the option of taking them out and displaying them in a child's room or playroom, then just wrap them around the battery pack and carefully push them into the jar, for safe keeping.

12 With strong glue, stick the battery pack to the inside of the jar lid. Make sure that the switch remains accessible. Once this has dried, wrap the battery with dark crepe paper to disguise it, arrange your glow worms in the jar and gently push the battery pack into the middle before securing the lid. To turn your glow-worms on and off, simply unscrew the lid and lift it out, giving you easy access to the switch.

Toy 'Snow' Globe

This is a really great project and very simple to make. There's nothing quite as magical as watching sparkling glitter whirl around a snow globe. Of course, you can use whatever colour glitter you like, depending on what toy you have chosen for your project.

This project offers a different take on the traditional snow globe. Choose a toy, or group of toys, that are no longer used by your children – plastic are best. Then chose a jar to suit their height and width.

You will need

* A plastic toy or toys of your choice

* Strong glue

* Glitter

* Water

* Spray paint (optional, for the lid)

1 Stick the toy/toys to the inside of the lid using your strong glue. You could also use superglue or a hot glue-gun. Set aside to dry.

2 To work out how much water you will need in your jar, you'll need to work by trial and error. The globe needs to be almost full, with only a very small air bubble at the top. I simply filled the jar with water, submerging the toys, letting the extra water push out.

3 Once you have the right amount of water, add a couple of sprinkles of glitter. You don't need very much to achieve a nice effect.

4 Submerge your toys. You will need to fix the lid in place with glue to ensure that no water leaks out. Rest the jar on a flat surface until the water has stilled. Gently wipe the neck of the jar until the glass is completely dry. Make sure the inside of the lid is also dry. Apply your strong glue to both surfaces. Screw the lid to the jar sealing the water inside. If you want to be extra vigilant, you can also apply a line of glue around the outside of the lid.

Presentation

I have spray-painted the lid silver, to give my jar an industrial feel, and to make it look more finished. Then I used permanent marker (you could use glass pens too) to decorate the top of the snow globe. This covers the small bubbble of water too.

Shark Attack!

This make teaches your kids about physics. It uses magnets, so it's a great way to show kids the force of magnetic attraction and teach them how magnets work.

I have chosen a shark scene for this project. However, you could create lots of different underwater scenes using the same basic principles. You could have a quivering seahorse, a goldfish, a manta ray or even a mermaid. The end result is really clever; the magnets will make the fish quiver and shake like the real thing!

You will need

* 5 or 6 round magnets, depending on the size of your jar

* Glass pebbles, blue stone chippings or small gravel/ pebbles

* A fish/shark shape (I used cut-outs from a nature magazine)

* Thread

* Clear sticky tape

* 1 metal paper-clip

* Strong glue

1 Stack the magnets one on top of the other, until they are about one-third of the depth of the jar. Stick them to the base of the jar using your strong glue.

2 Fill the space around the magnets with glass pebbles so that you can't see the magnets. Be careful not to place anything over the top of the magnets.

3 Find some suitable images for your jar, or draw them yourself! I have cut out a large shark's head from a magazine and then stuck it onto some thin cardboard to make it more robust. I have also cut out some little fishes, starfish and reef plants to decorate the base of the jar. It's these fish that my shark is trying to eat! You may notice that I have added some teeth to my shark. Apparently, the photographic cut out wasn't vicious enough (so said by my three-year-old son) and so I had to give it a big teethy mouth! Boys, eh?

4 This is the tricky bit. Cut a length of thread longer than the height of your jar. Tie one end of the thread onto the end of the paper-clip and slide the paper-clip onto the nose of the shark.

5 Use a small piece of clear tape to fix the thread to the back of the shark. Now, holding one end of the thread, hang the fish into the jar, just above the magnets, until you feel the magnets start to 'pull' on the clip. Place your fingers onto the thread, just at the point where the lid will be. This will tell you where to stick the thread to the jar lid. You want your shark to hang down so that it is just within the magnetic pull, but not touching the magnets. You may need to adjust your thread a couple of times to get it just right.

6 Once you have the right position, add some more tape around the thread, inside the lid of the jar, to secure it fully. When you shake the jar, your shark should shiver and shake just above the magnets!

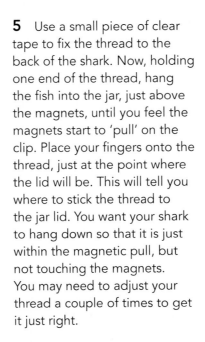

7 I have also used a paper stencil to add blue waves around the top of my jar. This has covered the lid and added a nice detail. You can read more about stencils and how to make them at the beginning of the book.

Aviary

The inspiration for this make was an old book that I found in a charity shop. The illustrations inside it were so vibrant and beautifully drawn. For this project I wanted to re-create something like an old-fashioned museum display, in which stuffed animals are perched in various poses, their names delicately inscribed on the glass of their capsules.

I found some great plastic trees and foliage for the display case and cut out my favourite parrot picture. You could use any type of tree-dwelling animal for this project.

Four or five of these in a row would make a great display on a child's shelf, you could use different species of parrots or birds, or even monkeys!

You will need

* A picture of a bird, or tree-dweller

* Green garden wire

* Some plastic toy trees and leaves

* Stiff thin cardboard

* Sharp scissors or a craft knife

* Glue stick

* Strong glue

* Silver spray paint

* Sticky tape

1 Cut out your chosen bird or animal roughly and, using glue stick, fix it to a piece of cardboard, smoothing out any lumps or air bubbles. Set aside to dry.

2 Accurately cut out the bird using sharp scissors or a craft knife.

3 Take a length of garden wire and bend it into an 'L' shape, to form the perch for the parrot. Tape or glue the wire onto the back of the bird.

4 Take a small piece of plastic foliage and, using strong glue, stick it to the end of the wire perch. Allow to dry.

5 Bend the other end of the wire around to make a circular base for the perch, pressing it down so that it will sit flat inside the lid of the jar. Use strong glue to stick it into place.

PLATYCERCUS PILEATUS.

  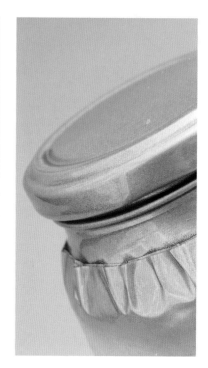

6 Add two or three trees around the perch, sticking them into the lid using strong glue. Don't worry too much if the trees stick out a little bit over the edge of your lid, as they are flexible enough to be bent inward when you place your aviary into your jar. Stick the parrot into place. Leave to dry.

7 Carefully place the aviary into the jar and secure the lid.

8 For a more authentic look, apply masking tape around the neck of the jar and spray paint the lid and the top of the jar silver. Cut out the name of your specimen and, using your glue stick, fix it to the front of the jar.

Five-a-Day Jar

I wanted to come up with a fun way to encourage my boys to eat their veggies, so I thought why not make a jar full of fruit and vegetables? The boys loved them and really enjoyed finding the fruit and vegetables that they had eaten and sticking them to the outside of the jar. I added some bright words of encouragement and even a 'bonus' area, where they could place any extra fruits or vegetables they had eaten.

The premise is simple. Fill up your jars with mini versions of all the fruit and vegetables that your children are regularly offered, or that you would like them to try. If you don't want to sew your veggies you can cut out photographs from magazines, or drawings. Just stick them to some card, cut them out and add the Velcro to the back.

You will need

* Mini fruit and vegetables (felt, small plastic toys, cut-outs)

* Velcro stickers – with adhesive

* Glass pens

1   Make your fruit and veg. If you are making them from felt, simply fold a small piece of felt in two and cut out the shape of your fruit. Using a fine thread in a matching colour, sew around the edges, leaving a little gap for stuffing. Stuff each shape then stitch the gap closed.

2   Stagger five velcro stickers down the front of the jar, stacking them evenly one on top of the other. Using your glass pens, draw colourful circles around the stickers, and add bright numbers so that your children can count off the fruit and veg as they go. Leave to dry.

3   If you want to, add a 'bonus' area on the back of the jar, where they can add any extra fruit or veg that they've eaten. Write words of encouragement around the jar, such as 'WOW!', 'WELL DONE!' and 'EXCELLENT!'

4   Fill the jar with the fruit and vegetables and look forward to healthy, happy, harmonious dinner times.

Terrarium

You may or may not be surprised to learn that there is a wealth of scientific research that proves the benefits of living with plants in our indoor environments. Interior plants can remove harmful airborne pollutants, they can control the humidity within the home, and they emit oxygen into their environment. Higher oxygen levels in the home make you feel alert, and can help you to concentrate.

Succulents are easy to care for, come in a range of breathtaking shades, shapes and sizes, and some of them can thrive with nothing but air.

You will need

* Succulent terrarium kit

* Large jar

1 Prepare the jar by washing it in hot water. Once dry, add a layer gravel to the base of the jar.

3 Add a layer of potting mix.

4 If you have any rooting plants in your kit, place them gently onto the soil so that the bottom on the plant is just sitting slightly below the surface.

5 Surround the plant and cover the potting mix with a layer of gravel. This should be finer than the bottom layer.

6 Add decorations such as shells, figurines and moss. You can pop an air plant on top, if you have enough room. Use long tweezers to move elements in the jar, if you can't reach in.

Generally you should keep your terrarium in a warm environment, but out of any strong direct sunlight. Give your plants some plant food every now and then, and water sparingly. You could also consider hanging your jar from a hook or from the ceiling.

Memory Jar

The idea of these Memory Jars is so sweet and simple that it has become a happy habit to make them in my home. The premise of the jar is very simple and easy to accomplish. Next time you go on holiday, take a special day trip or visit a new place, encourage your child to collect small things to bring home with them. It could be anything from ticket stubs, leaflets or receipts, to natural objects such as shells, flowers, leaves or stones. Anything that reminds them of the time they spent is great, providing it can fit in a jar! Alternatively, your child could draw a picture of something that they saw, which can be folded up and placed in the jar. You could also buy them a small souvenir to include in their memory display.

When you get home, or sometime after the event, you can arrange your items inside the jar. Make sure that you discuss each one with your child, talking about the happy times you had together as you place them. Once you are finished, you can write the date and location on the outside of the jar as a final touch. Your child will love to display their own special memories on a shelf in their room, or somewhere in the home where they can see it regularly. It will be something they look to whenever they need reassurance, and you will benefit from sharing the happy memories with them too!

Count Your Blessings Jar

The value of consciously 'counting your blessings' in order to achieve a positive mental outlook has been appreciated for quite a while now. The principle of counting your blessings is a genuinely beneficial one. However, counting them too often can reduce the benefits.

The idea is a simple one. Each time you feel grateful, or happy, or just pleasantly content, write the reason down, or what you were doing at the time, and you pop it in your 'Count Your Blessings' jar.

Finding a quiet moment in which to read through all your happy moments is a sure remedy for the blues. We all feel down at some point and find it hard to live in the present, appreciating what we have *now* instead of worrying about things that have happened in the past, or may happen in the future. It would be lovely to get into the habit of reading through the notes in your jar every month or so, to encourage a positive outlook. You could even do this as a family, asking your children if they'd like to write down something that they are grateful for. You might be surprised and delighted at some of their answers!

Weddings

As budget weddings become ever more popular, so too does the idea of DIY decorations, favours and flower arrangements. I've been to some absolutely stunning weddings, at which most of the décor was handmade by the bride, her friends and family. One such wedding used an eclectic mix of vintage china for the wedding breakfast, creating attractive tables that were both welcoming and very pretty.

From handmade decorations to homemade cakes, there are so many ways that you can save money on your wedding day. But it's not just about saving money! You will also have the benefit of having a 100 per cent unique wedding, because you have created it yourself. Give your friends and family the chance to contribute too, and they will be as proud as you are on the big day. Ask loved ones to start collecting jars well in advance. Most weddings are at least a year in the planning, so this shouldn't be a problem! You can use your saved jars for a range of items.

In this chapter I'll be showing you how to create atmosphere with colourful tea-lights, suggesting affordable yet beautiful flower arrangements, saving you time by combining favours with place settings, and there's also some fun ideas for your wedding guests. While I don't necessarily suggest that you use all of these makes in one wedding (might be a jar overload), there are many that you can use together, or suggest to a friend, or contribute to an upcoming big day.

Vintage Lace

If you've chosen a vintage theme for your wedding, or know someone that has, then lace is the perfect accessory to really set the scene. Versatile and readily available, lace can be used for all manner of trimmings. You can use lace as a quick and simple way of decorating a jar vase, or wrap it around smaller jars to create beautiful tea-light holders. In this project I will be suggesting how you can make both.

Vintage Lace Jar Vases

If you want to create a traditional vintage style, then look for lace that is white, cream or ivory. You do not need to spend a lot of money; simple pretty patterns are available online and in local haberdasheries. The more details and beading, sequins or flowers, the more expensive it is. However, for a vintage-style wedding, simple is best. If you are keeping your colours muted then the nude colours of lace are perfect.

The easiest way to buy lace is by the metre, or yard, choosing a wide ribbon. This type of lace is perfect for wrapping around jars. You can secure your lace with clear sticky tape at the back, or, if you want something more permanent, use a glue stick.

Vintage Lace Jar Tea Lights

I just love candles at a wedding. In the evening, as the lights go down, it's such a pretty sight to see lots of glowing candles on the tables, giving everything, and everyone, a romantic glow. If you've managed to collect a generous number of jars before the big day then you have the perfect tea-light holders for the event! Jars are a really safe way of displaying candles at a large party where dubious dance moves are likely to be practised and flammable hairspray is in abundance. Glass jars keep the naked flame encased, away from potential fire hazards. They are excellent for outdoor lighting as they will prevent any risk of your candle being blown out by the wind, and they are so easy to decorate.

1 Choose your preferred colour and style of lace and wrap a length around the jar. If you want a subtle, light colour then use one layer of lace. If you'd like a stronger colour use two.

2 Another option, is to place a darker coloured lace on the jar first and then cover it with a lighter shade. Your tea-lights will not only highlight the pattern of the intricate lace work, but will also cast a lovely colourful glow on the table around them.

If you love the idea of lace, but also want a powerful colour punch, then simply wrap some white lace over the top of your crepe paper. These really do look so pretty when they are lit!

When I planned my wedding, I had a strict budget to adhere to. We made a large saving on our flowers, which are often a very big part of a wedding budget. Apart from three bouquets, (one for me and one each for my two bridesmaids) all the flowers were provided loose, un-cut and un-arranged. This is where we made the saving. I ordered 200 beautiful roses, with absolutely massive blooms. The evening before the wedding, we collected the flowers, took them to our venue and began cutting them down to fit into my jar vases. The roses were so beautiful in themselves that they needed nothing else doing to them, apart from popping into the jars, which I had wrapped in lace, of course. I had so many comments throughout the day on how lovely all the flowers were.

Colour 'Pop' Tea-Lights

Dot these tealights along a walkway at a wedding. The effect is gorgeous and, once dusk comes, the lit candles offer a lovely burst of glowing colour.

It's a lovely idea to personalise your jars with a little tag or label, giving the date of the wedding or the surname of the happy couple. You could either paste this on, or attach it with some ribbon on a piece of card. Then, invite your guests to each take a tea-light home as a memento of the day.

You will need

* Brightly coloured crepe paper

* Glue stick

* Glass jars

1 Match your crepe paper colours to those of the wedding. Cut strips of crepe paper, the same width as the height of the jars. Wrap the paper around the jar to find the length you need. Remember to cut the crepe paper neatly, as any little tear will be highlighted once the candle is lit.

2 Smooth the paper around the jar and use your glue stick to secure the paper at the back. If you want a more permanent look, you could actually découpage the paper onto each jar using PVA glue mixed with a little water.

Wild Flowers

Although I've titled this project 'Wild Flowers' I don't actually mean wild flowers growing on public land, in meadows and on roadside. Happily, you can buy wild flowers from most florists, and not only will you be supporting a local business, but you'll be getting high quality flowers with a long shelf life and probably some plant food too. When I imagine wild flowers, they're often tall and straggly, with lots of lovely green foliage and brightly coloured petals. They are perfect for arranging in jars because, together with the repurposed jar, they give such a homely, country feel.

   Don't worry too much about actually 'arranging' your flowers; you want them to look natural, as if gathered quickly. Ensure you use lots of different heights of blooms to give depth and some different sizes of greenery to give a good texture. If you are using a short jar, don't be afraid to chop the flowers right down so that they sit nicely. If you'd like to leave the stems longer, why not try tying a length of ribbon around the bunch, above the top of the jar, so that they hold together?

Please don't pick wild flowers. Not only is it illegal in many countries, leaving you vulnerable to receiving a fine, but also, you will invariably end up with a floral arrangement with a much shorter life, as the flowers will not have been properly prepared for display. Some flowers, such as poppies, will actually start to wilt as soon as you pick them, leaving little point in actually doing it in the first place. You may risk disturbing a natural habitat, accidentally uprooting a rare plant, or just ruining a previously picturesque beauty spot.

Bride and Groom Peg Snow Globe

This is such a sweet present to give to the happy couple. It could also be given to flower girls, bridesmaids and even the groom's men, as a fun keepsake and memento of the special day. These are really easy to make and you can go to town on the design if you like, adding personalised details, different coloured dresses for bridesmaids and even mini-pegs for page boys and flower girls. You can add hair, lace veils, sparkling sequins and anything else you desire, just make sure that it's all securely stuck down!

You will need

* 1 wooden peg (pin)

* Marker pens in black and red (or your choice of colours)

* White paint such as acrylic or wood paint (not water-based)

* White paper, lace, sequins, or any other embellishments

* Strong glue (not water-based)

* White or sliver glitter

* Colourful card (card stock)

* Ribbon (optional)

* Glass pens (optional)

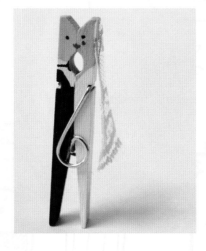

1 Design the bride and groom pegs. One side of the peg will be the bride, one side will be the groom (unless you're attending a same sex marriage, in which case duplicate the bride or groom design). The aim is to depict the couple kissing, therefore the tip of the pegs represents two heads touching. Simply draw dots for eyes and a red or pink mouth for the bride. Then colour the rest of your pegs (from the tip, or neck, downward) to resemble the bridal outfits.

2 Add veils, tiaras, sequins or lace as you see fit, making sure that you don't add anything that will dissolve in water once you fill the jar!

3 Using your strong glue, attach the feet of the bride and groom pegs to the inside lid. They will be standing upright once the jar is upside down. Leave the glue to set hard.

4 Add water to the jar, and work out how much you will need to fill it, by submerging your peg and adjusting the water level accordingly. You want the jar almost full, with only the smallest air bubble at the top.

5 Use a hole punch to punch holes from coloured card. These will be confetti.

6 Add a pinch of glitter and your confetti to the water in the jar. Secure the lid, using hot glue or strong glue. Once the jar is sealed add another layer of glue around the outside of the rim for extra protection. If the glue is visible once dried, add a pretty ribbon around the neck of the jar to cover it.

7 You can personalise these snow globes by writing the surname of the bridal couple, the date of the wedding, or a simple message on your jar with glass pens.

Favours and Place Settings

Most of us can appreciate how much work there is to be done when organising a wedding. We all know that making beautiful items to customise the day takes time. Keeping this in mind, I have created this project, which combines two essential components of a perfect wedding day in one simple make. Not only can you use these jars as place settings for the wedding breakfast, but your guests can take them home as wedding favours too. They will all be personalised, as each jar feature a guest's name and you can fill them as you like. Old-fashioned traditional sweets (candies) make a really colourful filling, or strawberry bon-bons, chocolates, mints or mini macaroons.

I have chosen to fill my jars with traditional sweets, but I have also added a tea-light underneath, so the place setting has a dual purpose. To make an attractive tea-light holder you can wrap your jar in a variety of materials, crepe paper, lace, simple ribbons, or hessian, as I've suggested below.

You will need

* Hessian (Burlap)

* Scissors

* Glue stick

* Colourful sweets (candies)

* Card (card stock)

* Stamps

* Ribbon

* Tea-light

1 Use your jar as a guide by placing it on the hessian and marking the height with a pencil. Now wrap the hessian around the jar to measure the length. Cut out the hessian, leaving a little extra length to overlap at the back of the jar.

2 Take a piece of card and fold it in half. Draw half a heart shape on it and cut out. Once you open this up you will have a perfectly symmetrical heart-shaped template for your hessian. Place on the material and draw around it with a pencil.

3 Cut out the heart. It is easier to do this if you fold the material in half along the centre line of the heart.

4 Wrap hessian around the jar, using a glue stick to secure it at the back. Place your tea-light at the base and then pile in some sweets.

5 To create your place settings, cut out a rectangle of card and use your stamps (or write by hand if you have neat writing!) to print out your guest's names. Use a hole-punch at one end and string your name card onto your jar using a thin ribbon.

6 You can provide these jars without lids if you want to, as, after all, the lid cannot be used while the candle is lit! However, it is handy to have a lid to keep the sweets and the candle in place. If you'd like to use lids, the best way to decorate them is to use spray paint, as it will cover them evenly and will be much quicker than painting them individually. Alternatively, you could use some wedding themed Washi tape, which is very quick and easy to apply.

Lemonade

Whenever I think of a quintessential summer garden party, the memory of drinking homemade, cloudy and refreshing lemonade always comes to mind. Summer garden weddings have always been popular, and this project goes hand in hand with the tempting idea of a ceremony that takes place outside.

Set out a table of traditional lemonade, with retro paper straws and cute jars instead of glasses. Use glass jars and you will have a full set of quirky glasses for your reception drinks. You could even add the 'cheeky option' of a splash of something a little stronger, if you want your guests to be really cheerful.

You will need

* Glass jars

* Black-board (chalkboard) paint

* White chalkboard pen

1 To create a set of bride and groom 'glasses' paint a black heart onto the front of each jar and allow to dry.

2 Personalise the jars by adding a message, or name with white chalkboard pen.

3 As a finishing touch, pop a colourful paper straw into each jar and display somewhere prominent at the event. For an artistic touch, I particularly like the shape of red lips (bride) and a moustache (groom) for a quirky detail.

A Jar of Happily Ever After

Ask your guests to write a short piece of marriage advice, humour, or sentiment, and pop it into the 'Happily Ever After Jar'. It really is as simple as that. Provide a pack of colourful cards, paper and pens and your jar will look really inviting when it's full. You and your husband can share a special moment reading through all of the loving messages, marriage tips and thoughtful pointers.

There are times in every relationship where we struggle to really appreciate and value what we have. It's hard to be constantly mindful of how lucky we are. Your 'Happily Ever After Jar' will be there if times get tough and you need a little pick me up. If you ask people for

their earnest advice, you will be surprised at what you receive. Most people love to give their opinions on things, given half a chance, so don't be surprised if your jar is overflowing by the time the night is over!

Placing a 'Happily Ever After Jar' at your wedding is asking for the support of your friends, family and loved ones right from the get go, and what better start could a marriage have?

Floating Flowers

These floating flowers are so easy to put together and look so very beautiful. They're perfect for weddings, or as table decorations at any occasion. You could also use a bowl to display a group of flowers, with some floating candles dotted in-between. And remember, you don't have to wait for guests to visit or to host a dinner party to use these decorations.

I can imagine these jars lined up across the front of the bride and groom's table, a colourful line of beautiful blooms. Alternately, they would look great lined along the centre of long tables, grouped together in the middle of round tables, or simply dotted around a wedding venue. You can use lots of the same flower, roses, for example, all in the same colour, or to match the wedding bouquet flowers. Add some vibrant green leaves, just popping out of the top of each jar. The deep green rose leaves provide a wonderful contrast to the soft peachy petals.

Gerberas are perfect for this project, as are dahlias, hydrangeas, mums and spider mums, among others. Anything with a large, round and colourful bloom will look perfect.

Tea-Lights

Glass jars are just perfect for making tea-light holders. They can be used inside and out, as the glass of the jar will protect your candle from being extinguished by the wind. The flame of your tea-light is safely enclosed within the jar. Glass tea-light holders are easy to decorate, inexpensive, and the soft, romantic glow when dotted around a room is just magical.

 In this chapter we use a variety of methods to jazz up plain glass jars. From simple glass pens, to luxurious woolly knits, with a smattering of découpage, glitter and vintage paper along the way, all your crafty skills will be called into play. The first make is a spectacular garden chandelier. It's one of my favourite makes and looks really fabulous hanging in the garden.

Warning
I would never endorse leaving candles burning while you are not present, or where young children or animals are likely to be. **Never, ever leave candles unattended.**

 Sometimes the neck and top of the glass can get very hot, so always pick them up from the base, where it is usually cold enough to touch. And lastly, please keep them well out of the reach of your children.

Garden Chandelier

I found inspiration for this project at the side of the road. Literally, I was walking home when I found two discarded chandeliers, rusty and dusty, wet from the rain, and perfect for a restoration project.

As soon as I saw them I had a vision of garden lanterns. They were ideal for hanging from trees, as they already had a hook at the top, and I was sure that, after being cleaned up, they would be perfect to spray with paint. I have provided a lot of detail about how I prepared the chandeliers; it's important to always prepare properly before restoration. The ground work is dull, granted, but it is certainly worth it for the finished result. Chandeliers that you find in thrift or charity shops can be prepared similarly.

To make the Garden Chandelier, you will need:

* A salvaged chandelier

* Pliers

* Wire cutters

* Sandpaper (heavy grade glass paper) and dusting cloth

* Small screwdriver

* Spray paint

* Glue stick

* Strong glue

* Thin card (card stock) or paper

* White spirit/Paint thinner

* A cotton bud/Q-tip

1 Strip the chandelier of its electrical wires and fixings. Use your pliers and wire cutters to cut off the electrical lead at the top of the chandelier. Remove any chains, unless they are in good condition and you would like to keep them for hanging.

2 Remove the bulb fittings. They are usually plastic or metal. If they are metal, then you may need to use a small screwdriver to prise open the tiny 'clips' on each side of the fitting that hold it in place. Most fittings are screwed onto the main frame of the chandelier, so always twist it to see if it budges. If it's too tight or rusty, use your pliers.

3 Cut the electrical wire beneath the bulb fitting; this should allow you to pull the fitting completely off. If you can, pull the wires out of the chandelier, but don't worry if they are stuck fast, as they won't be seen.

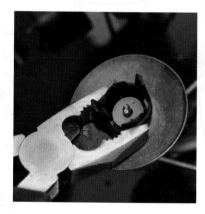

4 If there's a small dish, or plate that sits underneath the fitting, which is now loose, tighten it. If not, simply fix the plates back into place with a hot glue gun, or strong glue.

5 Make sure the chandelier is clean and free of grit and dust before you paint it. If it is rusty in any areas, then rub it down with a coarse sandpaper. The paint should cover up the rust.

6 Cover the area in which you will be painting to protect it from receiving an unwanted makeover. It is best to do this outside, if you can. Choose the colour you want the chandelier to be, and get spraying. Chandeliers look great in bright, bold colours, as well as white and cream.

7 I wanted my chandelier to be a bright pink, so I sprayed it white first, to make sure that the dark metal wouldn't dull the finished colour. Once painted, set the chandelier aside to dry.

8 Decide which jars best fit the chandelier. To do this, place the jars onto the plates until you find a shape you're happy with. It looks nice if the jars are the same width, or just a little wider than your plates.

9 I wanted my chandelier to emit diffused light, so I sprayed the inside of each jar lightly with white paint. To do this, I held the nozzle of the spray paint a couple of inches away from the neck of the jar, and sprayed directly into it, using short bursts.

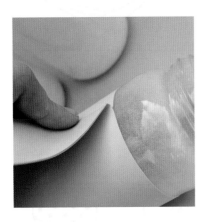

of the paper so that when you cut it out, the pattern will be repeated four times across your sheet.

12 I have chosen a simple tulip shape, with a leaf on one side. Cut your pattern out.

IMPORTANT: Remember to only cut *below* the line you have drawn, starting at one side and cutting across to the other. The bottom half of your template should now fall away.

Repeat this process until you have a template for each jar.

13 Lightly apply some glue stick around the edges of the design. Wrap it around the jar, ensuring that all of the edges are pressed down, so that the paint doesn't travel underneath them. Also make sure that the rest of the jar is covered, so that the paint doesn't mark it. Repeat for each jar.

14 Hold the jar at arms' length, so that the base of the jar is pointing away from you. Lightly spray the lower half, holding the can 20–30 cm/8–12 in away. This should give an even coverage without the risk of the paint becoming too thick and seeping under the paper. Cover the base of the jar with paint.

15 Cut off any excess paper that is above the rim of your jar and set upside down to dry. Repeat for all of your jars. Resist the temptation to peel off the templates too early, as you could smudge the edges of your design.

16 Once dry, peel off the paper, or, soak it in some water and rub it off with your fingers. Do not use anything abrasive to wash the paper off, or you risk scratching the paintwork.

17 Study the design for smudges. If you find any, they can be easily removed with a little white spirit/paint thinner on the end of a cotton bud.

10 To make a template for the pattern to be applied to the outside of the jars, wrap a sheet of thin card or paper around the jar, folding it where the paper meets, to mark the circumference of the jar and trim on the foldline. Mark the length of the jar with a fold all the way across the paper and trim.

11 Fold the card or paper in half lengthwise and in half again but not including the excess paper in the folding. Draw your pattern at one end

18 Using strong glue, super glue or a hot glue gun apply a line of glue around the rim of the plate, and to the base of your jar. Place each jar into position, making sure that it is sitting straight.

IMPORTANT: Some of these glues will dissolve the paint on your jar, so make sure you only apply glue to the base, where it won't be seen.

19 Set aside to dry completely. If there is a visible line of glue around the base of your jars, you can always spray them with another layer of paint to cover it, making sure that you cover the rest of the jars so that you don't ruin your design.

Floating Candles

Floating candles have been popular for a long time. They are a visual display that never goes out of fashion. There's just something about the way the light of the candle plays on the surface of the water that is very appealing. Floating candles can be displayed in bowls, vases, shallow dishes, and even jam jars. I once went to a wedding that had giant cocktail glasses on the tables, each filled with polished stones, water and floating candles. The effect was magnificent. It should only take you a few minutes to pull this project together. Submerging things in water can make even the dullest of items take on a magical, ethereal colour. Next time you're having guests, don't overlook this wonderful idea for a quick and easy table display.

You will need

* Glass jars

* Floating candles

* Large pebbles, gravel, sand, shells, glass pebbles, marbles, heavy beads, and pretty much anything that sinks

1   Cover the base of the jar with decorative items. Don't fill it too high, you need to leave room for some water and the candle. About halfway up your chosen jar is perfect.

2   Fill with water. You can also experiment with coloured water, using food colouring or water-based paint. Float a candle on top.

Vintage Paper

This is another great up-cycling project. Using old papers, music sheets and maps, you can create these classic tea-light holders for very little cost. Older, slightly yellowed paper helps create a vintage theme. Children's picture books with classic illustrations are also an excellent choice.

Often we may frown at cutting up books, but I believe that if they're not being used then it's better to give them a fresh lease of life.

You will need

* Old papers

* Glass jars

* Glue

1 Simply cut your paper to the right size and glue it to the jar.

Ideas for Vintage Paper Jars

Tiny Hearts
Use a heart-shaped cutter to stamp a line of hearts around the top of the paper. The light will look lovely shining through them.

Large Cut-Out
Cut a shape in the middle of your paper; a heart, a star, or anything you fancy, to let the light shine through.

Old Map Trail
If you are using an old map, you could try using a thick needle or thin nail to poke mini holes through to create a shape, or route. You can even personalise it to highlight a special place that is close to your heart.

Highlights
You could add some decorative highlights to your paper, using a metallic pen, stickers or glitter. Sheet music looks lovely with a metallic detail drawn across it, or just the odd silver or bold letter here and there!

A Secret Message
If you are using a passage from a book to decorate your jar, try highlighting certain words. You can use this method to write a secret message, a sentimental phrase or even a famous quote.

Dipped Glitter Glam

If you want to add a touch of luxury to your next dinner party, then look no further! These dipped glitter glam candle jars really do add a lot of sparkle to any occasion. There are plenty of different designs to be created, from keeping it simple with one colour, to stripes and glitter shapes. I've decided to create a display using three colours, three jars and two different designs. Use whatever jars you have to hand, as well as your favourite colours. I have used a fine grade glitter as I like the effect.

When I first started experimenting with this project, I wondered if the colours might merge. I also wasn't sure that I could create a crisp line between colours. How wrong could I be!

You will need

* Glitter (any colours you like)

* Glue stick

* Fixing spray, clear spray-on varnish or clear spray paint, to 'fix' or 'set' the design

* Masking tape

1 My first design has a simple line running around the jar, so that it is high on one side and low on the other. This really does make your jar look like it has been 'dipped' in glitter. Using glue, draw a line all the way around the jar, starting around two-thirds of the way up the jar, then lowering to around the one-third point at the opposite side before gently arching back up to the original starting point. You should be able to clearly see the line of glue as you draw it on.

2 Glue all of the glass below the line. Try to create a smooth finish with no gaps or lumps. A glue stick is perfect for this.

3 Protect the work surface with a large piece of newspaper to catch any excess glitter. Make a fold all the way across this paper before you start. This will help you pour the glitter back into its pot later.

4 Hold your jar in one hand, at a slightly tilted angle, so that when the glitter hits the glass it rolls downward. Now, shake glitter slowly over the lower half of the jar, turning the jar as you go, until it is all covered. Tap the top of the jar to shake off any excess. Don't worry if there are small bits of glitter stuck to the top of the jar; you can wipe them off later. Set the jar aside to dry.

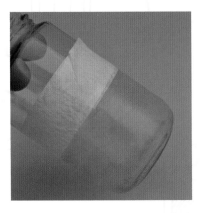

5 For the striped design, apply a length of masking tape around a jar and level with the base. Use your glue stick to cover the area below the tape with glue, making sure that the glue runs right up to and slightly over, onto the tape.

6 Apply glitter as before. Once the lower section is covered, and you have shaken off any excess, remove the masking tape. Leave to dry for at least 1 hour.

7 Apply another length of masking tape, so that the lower edge is 2.5 cm/1 in from the top of the white glitter. You can make this gap smaller or larger, depending on how wide you would like your purple stripe to be. Carefully apply a layer of glue to the section of glass below the tape. Make sure you rub the glue right up to the line of white glitter, but being careful not to rub any of the white glitter off.

8 Apply purple glitter as before. Hold the jar so that it is horizontal, parallel to the table or the floor beneath you. This should stop the glitter from moving down over the white section. Apply glitter as before, but being careful to keep it level. You will need to overlap the purple glitter ever so slightly onto the white layer, to ensure that there are no gaps. Once your have covered the middle layer, tap the glass to shake off any excess, and put it aside to dry for another hour.

9 Repeat steps 7 and 8 to apply the final stripe of glitter. Leave to dry. With a tissue wipe any excess from the top of the jars. Fix the glitter, so that it doesn't rub off. You can use fixer spray, clear spray paint or clear spray-on varnish.

Découpage

I have used this technique multiple times and happily it is great for jars. The way that tissue paper diffuses the light of a candle is just stunning.

Découpage uses layers of paper stuck together using a mixture of PVA glue and water. I like to use two parts glue to one part water, as this gives you a fairly thick liquid, which is wet enough to soak through the paper. I have chosen to use plain crepe paper for this project, so that I can create my own designs by cutting out simple shapes. My design has been inspired by lavender flowers as I love the colour, as well as the scent. It would be a lovely touch to make this design and then finish it off with a lavender-scented candle to burn inside.

I have used a square jar for this project. However, any jar will work.

You will need

* Crepe paper in the following colours: White, Green, Light Purple, Dark Purple

* PVA glue

* Water

* Soft paintbrush

* Hole punch

1 Cut a long length of white crepe paper that is the same width as the height of the jar. We are not going to cover the neck or the base of the jar, so it just needs to be wide enough to cover the sides. The white paper will be the design background.

2 We are going to cover one side or section of the jar at a time. Place the jar on its side and paint the glass side that is facing you with PVA mixed with water as detailed above. Place your paper onto the glass, making sure that it is lying level and straight with the base. Paint over the paper gently, with more PVA mix. Do not press too hard or you risk tearing the paper. Do not worry if your paper looks wrinkly, as this will disappear once it has dried.

3 Repeat on each side until you have covered the jar in the white paper. Set aside to dry slightly, while you prepare the rest of your design.

4 For the lavender flowers, fold the light and dark purple papers together three or four times. Using a hole punch, punch a generous pile of purple circles.

5 Cut strips of green paper 2–3 mm/$^1/_8$ in wide for the stems.

6 Glue green strips spacing them at random intervals around the base of the jar, for the stems. Leave enough space above the strips to add flowers, and vary the height of the stems. Leave to dry.

7 I found the easiest way to apply the flower circles is to pick them up in groups with the end of the moist paintbrush, stick them onto the jar, and then paint over them. Apply them randomly, as each flower should look wild and different!

8 If you want to lengthen your jar's shelf life, apply a layer of matt varnish once the design has dried.

Crochet

Crochet is a new passion of mine. Happily, when I tried out making little crochet jackets for my jars, they looked so sweet. I have used some pretty stand-out wool for these jar covers, though this make also looks attractive in neutral beiges, creams and browns. In fact, you can make them to suit any décor.

They are great used as handy little containers, pen holders or change jars, but I think that they look best with a candle inside them. As I have used the single (double) crochet stitch, there are plenty of little gaps for the light to shine through. There are plenty of tutorial videos on the web that explain how to crochet, so have a look there if this is a craft you're unfamiliar with. This project uses a very simple method.

You will need

* Wool (the wool packaging should state what size crochet hook to use)

* Crochet hook

* Darning needle

1 Tie a slip knot onto the crochet hook. Make a row of chain stitches until you have a rope the same length as the height of the jar. The easiest way to gauge this is to hold the chain next to the jar. Remember to note the number of chain stitches that you made.

2 Once you have the correct number of chain stitches, turn the work and stitch back along the chain, using a single crochet stitch. Count the stitches as you go.

3 Keep going, adding row after row until you have a rectangle of crochet that's just shorter than the circumference of the jar. Cast off the crochet. Stopping just short of the circumference length will mean that your crochet sits tight around the jar, instead of sagging.

4 Use a darning needle to sew the cast-on and cast-off ends of crochet together. Push the jacket onto the jar.

Glass Pens

The candle inside the jar is absolutely essential in bringing out the beauty of these pens. Suddenly wonderful colours burst out from the glass.

It's easy to create a 'stained glass' effect with these pens, as most of the packs come with a thick black paint pen that you can use to draw outlines. Once the black outlines are dry, you can fill the patterns in with the thinner, translucent colours. I have made two versions, the simple zig-zag pattern and a 'stained glass' effect design. For this latter design, I simply started with a flower in the middle of the jar, and worked my way outward, covering the jar in shapes of all types. The colours are thin, so I added two layers of colour to get the final effect. They'd make a great project to do with the kids on a wet afternoon. Just add candles to bring a little sunshine into the room!

Parties

Each year I host any number of parties. At the time that I suggest them, they sound like a great idea, and I'm full of enthusiasm with ideas for food, entertainment and pretty decorations. However, the closer the party gets, the more I find myself thinking *what an earth have I done?* My husband wonders why I worry, but he's wise enough not to voice his opinions aloud when I am in my pre-party mood. The answer to his question is simple. I worry because I want everyone to have a good time, to enjoy the atmosphere I've created, to love the food and drink I've made. That's not too much to ask, is it?

I love it really. Over the years I've found that making careful choices and choosing dishes that can be prepared in one pot, made in advance or are very simple, are the key to party success. In this chapter I'll be providing you with two great time-saving party ideas for adult gatherings.

It's a whole different ball game for kids' parties. When it comes to a children's birthday party, I'm less worried about recipes, drinks and aperitifs and more concerned about my floor, the new sofa and my sanity. But I do want the kids to have a good time. So, in this chapter are some truly amazing cakes, excellent goody bags (or jars), some spooky Halloween tea-lights and even homemade bubbles. What more could any child want?

Halloween Jars

These went down so well at my last Halloween party that I just had to include them here. The jars each took me less than ten minutes to make, and I know that they will be re-appearing every Halloween for years to come. There are hundreds of spooky tea-light holders to choose from when shopping for Halloween decorations, but why buy them when you can make them yourself?

You will need

* Orange and white spray paint

* Black water-based paint

* PVA glue

* Black permanent markers, or black glass paint

* Pencil

* Cotton buds (Q-tips)

* Washing up liquid

1 To make the ghost design, spray the inside of each jar with a light misting of white paint. Try not to apply it too thick, as you want your candle to be able to shine through once you're finished. Allow to dry.

2 For the ghost face, use the black marker, or black glass paint to draw two 'arches' for the eyes. Fill them in with black.

3 Now use the black pen to draw eyelashes from the lower edge of each eye, as if the pen is dripping down the jar. Make a larger arch for the mouth. Add two small thin lines for the nostrils. You may need to apply a couple of coats to get a really solid black.

4 To make the pumpkin face, spray the inside of the jar lightly with orange paint. Allow to dry.

5 Draw a pumpkin face on the jar. I have made triangular eyes, and a wide mouth with pointy teeth. Fill in the shapes using the black marker or black glass paint.

6 To make the skull face, spray the inside of the jar lightly with white paint. Allow to dry.

7 Mix one part black water-based paint with one part PVA glue. Now use this mixture to cover the outside of the jar completely. Allow to dry.

8 Use a damp cotton bud soaked in warm soapy water, start by rubbing off a circle toward the top of the jar. Wait a few seconds for the paint to soften, and then wipe the area firmly. This is the head.

10 Use the cotton bud to remove the paint *inside* your large circle, but leave the shapes of the eye sockets and nostrils black.

can be tricky, so soften the paint first by wetting the area slightly. Then use something small and hard, such as the end of a matchstick, to push off the black paint. Add another row of teeth, and then another strip below for the lower jaw.

12 Once you have your skull shape you can give your jar a coat of clear, matt varnish or use fixer spray for longevity, if you wish.

These are great for decorating your windowsill, lighting the way for trick-or-treaters or even casting some spooky shadows in your garden at night! If you want to get the kids involved, and reap the benefits of a quiet Halloween game in the process, why not prepare the insides of your jars in advance, and then let the children decorate one each at the party? There could even be a prize for the most gruesome lantern at the end!

9 Now, draw two circles for the eye sockets inside the first circle. Add two thin ovals for nostrils.

11 For the jaw, rub away a strip at the base of the head. Remove all the black paint within this strip. Under the jaw, remove lots of little squares, these are your teeth. These

Lego Goody Jars

Lego-themed parties are becoming increasingly popular for boys and girls, so for this project, I wanted to make party bags to give to the kids at the end of a party that have a lego theme. You can pop lots of lovely treats inside the jars, including a lego treat.

    The best jars to use for this make are those with a wide body and a tall lid, to replicate the dimensions of a 'Lego' man's head. Although, after you've sprayed them yellow and added a face, people will get the idea! Set these out at the party, somewhere where they can't be knocked over, and you can also use them as a decoration. These really are fun to make, great to receive and look totally cool (especially the one with shades).

You will need

* Bright yellow spray paint
* Black and red marker pens

1 Thoroughly clean the jars inside and out so that they are gum and grease free. Screw the lids on tightly. In a well ventilated area protected with newspaper, spray the jars all over, except for the bases. Spray from every angle, so that they are completely yellow. You may need to apply two coats. Allow the paint to dry for at least 24 hours, as there will be slightly thicker areas gathered around the lid.

2 To add the 'Lego' faces, be as inventive as you like and use the black pen for all the details, to make them realistic. You will need your red pen for any girl Lego heads (lipstick, of course!) Keep the designs simple and neat.

3 Unscrew the jars and fill with awesome party treats. You could also add a little note saying something like this:

Thanks for coming to (name of child)'s Lego party. I hope you had fun and enjoy your Lego Goody Jar treats. Once I'm empty, pop your little Lego bits in me and I'll keep them safe for you!

Rainbow Cakes

Great to look at, even better to eat, and packed into 'oh so cute' baby jars, these rainbow cakes are the most fabulous baking project for your children's party.

These mini cakes are extremely practical, limiting the sugar intake of children. They're easy to make and can be made in advance and stored in the refrigerator. The sponge won't dry out because *it's in a jar*. All you need to do on party day is whip up some cream, pipe it on the top and sprinkle on some sparkly candies.

It really is great to see the kids' faces when you bring out these colourful cakes, especially as they cut in with their spoon and see the wonderful circle patterns on the inside. Have your camera ready!

You will need

* Vanilla sponge cake or vanilla cupcake mix

* Edible food colour in bright shades

* Baby jars

* Whipped cream or butter icing (frosting)

* Sprinkles

1 Pre-heat the oven to a slightly lower temperature than advised (this is to stop the cake from browning around the edges). Make up a sponge mix as directed on the packet. Divide the mixture equally between four different bowls.

2 Add a few drops of food colour to each bowl. I chose red, blue, yellow and green. Make them vibrant.

3 Add 1 tablespoon of one colour to each jar, spreading it out before adding the next colour. Repeat to add a spoonful of each colour until each jar is half filled.

4 Place on a baking tray and place in the oven. Use the time stated on the packet as a guide, but check regularly for browning. If the cakes start to brown on the edge, but are raw in the middle, turn the oven temperature down. Insert a long metal skewer into the middle of each cake. If it comes out clean, the cakes are baked. Allow to cool.

5 If the cakes have risen above the rim of the jar, use a knife to slice off their tops so that they are level. You will see a great pattern inside. Once they have cooled completely, cover with cling film (plastic wrap) and refrigerate until you need them. These will be fine in the refrigerator for 2–3 days.

6 On party day, bring the cakes back to room temperature by taking them out of the fridge a few hours before your guests arrive. Pipe on you're the icing and decorate with sprinkles.

Homemade Bubbles

Every kid (old and young) likes to blow bubbles. In this project you get to design your own bubble jars to suit the theme of your party. You can even make bubble wands, customised to suit your theme.

Baby jars are ideal for this make, they are the perfect size for small hands and your guests can take them home as a memento of the party. Add labels, glass paint or glitter, and decorate the lids with Washi tape, paint, stick-on jewels or even small toys.

For a dinosaur party stick mini dinosaurs to the lids, and use green pipe cleaners for bubble wands. You could glue mini toy soldiers or even ballerinas for a dance lover. Add a few drops of food colouring if you want coloured bubbles too!

You will need

* Baby jars with lids

* Spray paint, for the lid

* Small plastic toys (optional)

* Pipe cleaners (chenille sticks)

* Glycerine

* Washing up liquid (try and get a clear, colourless soap if you can)

* Food dye (optional)

* Glitter (optional)

* Glue stick (optional)

1 In a well ventilated area, protected with newspaper, spray paint the lids, using your chosen colour. Once dry, glue your chosen toys to the lids.

2 Shape the pipe cleaners into bubble wands. I wanted a little glitter pot to hold my wands, so I have covered another jar with glue and then with glitter for this purpose (see 'Dipped Glitter Glam').

3 Mix up the bubble solution. Use one jar as '1 part' in the following recipe: (should make enough to fill 8 baby-sized jars)

2 parts clear washing up liquid
1 part glycerine
4 parts water
Pour everything into a bowl and stir well.

4 Divide the mixture between the jars. Screw on the lids and display your pretty party treats.

Lemon Posset

Lemon posset has a texture so dreamily creamy, and a flavour that is deliciously tangy. This dessert has become one of my favourite supper party recipes. They're quick to make too, using just one pan.

Lemon posset is perfect for serving in jars. It is very rich so you only need to serve a small portion per person. Baby jars are just the right size.

It's a nice touch to add some lemon zest to the top for colour, or a grating of dark (bittersweet) chocolate, for contrast.

You will need

To fill six baby sized jars:

* 600 ml/1 pint double (heavy) cream

* 150 g/5 oz caster (superfine) sugar

* 2 large lemons – zest and juice only

1 Add the cream and sugar to a pan and heat gently until it slowly comes to a boil. Allow to bubble gently for 3 minutes, stirring until the sugar is dissolved.

2 Remove from the heat and allow to cool for about 10 minutes. Now add the lemon juice and most of the zest, saving some for the tops, and mix well.

3 Pour into the jars and sprinkle on the rest of your zest. Leave to cool and then refrigerate until chilled. These will usually take a couple of hours to set.

Cocktail Party

Ideal for adult parties, these cocktail jars look fabulous lined up at the (homemade) bar! With their bright and colourful contents already added, all your guests have to do is choose their favourite and add a measure of alcohol. But what about a cocktail mixer, I hear you cry? No problem. Simply screw on the jars lid and get shaking! Your party goers will love the novelty of these cocktail jars, as well as the fun of shaking up their own drink. For a personal touch, you can add a little chalkboard circle for them to write their names on. I don't know about you, but I'm always losing my glass at parties.

You will need

* Colourful straws

* Lemon, limes and cocktail cherries

* Cocktail umbrellas

* Mixer sticks

* Fruit on a stick

* Cocktail muddler – if you haven't got one of these, a wooden spoon, or a wooden pestle (from pestle and mortar) is fine.

The serving suggestions for your jam jar cocktails can be as elaborate as you like, you can even draw up a chalkboard 'menu' for your guests to choose from. Have some spare jars at the side of your table to fill with cocktail umbrellas, fruit on sticks and, of course, make sure you have plenty of ice. Fresh limes, lemons and cocktail cherries aplenty, your guests will be getting into the party mood faster than you can say 'Happy Hour!'

I have chosen three cocktail recipes, however, there are hundreds of recipes online, if your favourite isn't here. In order to stop your cocktails becoming too potent, supply your guests with a shot measure, so that they can add their alcohol responsibly!

photo © puchkovo48 / Shutterstock.com

To make Mojito jars

* Dark rum

* Fresh mint leaves

* Limes

* Sugar syrup

* Soda water

1 Take a handful of mint leaves and scrunch them up between your hands, so that they start to release the scent and flavour. Place them in the base of the jar.

2 Add the juice of half a lime and a shot of sugar syrup (25 ml/1 fl oz)

3 Use a mixer stick to swirl the liquid around with the leaves. Set up a small sign that tells guests to add ice and a shot of rum, replace the lid of the jar and shake. Unscrew the lid and top up with soda water.

To make English Garden jars

* Gin

* Apple juice

* Limes

* Sugar syrup

* Mint

* Cucumber

1 Add a shot of sugar syrup (25 ml/1 fl oz) and the juice of half a lime to each jar. Take a few torn leaves of mint and throw them in. Add two slices of cucumber and top up with apple juice, until about two-thirds full. This should leave room for ice and a shot of gin to be added by your guests later. Stir the mixture and set aside.

2 Write instructions for guests to add ice and a shot of gin, before replacing the jar lid and giving their cocktail a shake.

To make Raspberry Collins jars

* Vodka

* Fresh raspberries

* Lemons

* Sugar syrup

* Soda water

1 Add approximately 9 raspberries to your jar. Use you cocktail 'muddler' to squish them lightly.

2 Add the juice of half a lemon and a shot (25 ml/1 fl oz) of sugar syrup, then stir briefly.

3 Write instructions for your guests telling them to add a scoop of ice and a shot of vodka. Replace the lid and shake the jar. Remove the lid and top up with soda water.

Christmas

I love the festive season. And best of all I love the opportunity to cover every surface of my home in fairy lights, glitter, tea lights, tinsel and fake snow. There'll probably be a few pom-poms too! Christmas is the best time to snuggle up with your loved ones, toasty and warm inside the house, surrounded by festive candles and decorations.

In this chapter you will find a great project to make *with* your kids as well as a great project to make *for* your kids, along with festive berries, napkin découpage and a silhouette snow town. There is also a stunning idea for a Christmas table centrepiece.

Wrapping Paper Tea Lights

This festive and fun project is one to make with your children. They will love to sort through your wrapping paper scraps to find pictures and patterns that they like. It will give them an excellent opportunity to practise their cutting and gluing skills, as well as encouraging them to be creative with their designs. Try to avoid foil paper and anything too thick, as these will be difficult to stick onto the jar. Cheap and cheerful, thin and bright paper is the best.

There are so many different designs you could make with these jars, and they look really lovely dotted around the house at Christmas. If you want to add a special finishing touch to your tea-light holders, you could glue a line of gold or foil ribbon around the top of the jar. This also covers up the rim of the jar. Please make sure that there is no ribbon overhanging the rim of the jar, as this could be a fire hazard.

You will need

* Christmas wrapping paper scraps

* White crepe paper, or tissue paper

* PVA glue and water

* Soft paintbrush

* Fine Christmas ribbon, for finishing touches

1 Look through your wrapping paper and choose the designs and characters that you like. Cut them out as close to the edges as you can.

2 Cut out some small details too such as snowflakes, holly leaves or stars. These can be placed around the jar to complement your main design.

3 Mix three parts PVA glue with one part water. Paint a layer of glue onto the glass, stick on your design and then paste over the top of it with more glue. Once you are happy with the position of your cuttings, set your jar aside to dry slightly. Cover your PVA mixture with cling film (plastic wrap) so that it doesn't dry out.

4 Once the cuttings are mostly dry, wrap the jar in a layer of white crepe paper so that it looks white and snowy. This will also diffuse the light from the candle, so that your jar glows nicely when lit.

5 Cut your crepe paper to the right size. Cover the entire jar in your PVA mix. Wrap the crepe paper around the jar and apply a layer of PVA mixture over the top. Don't worry if the paper looks wrinkly, as this should disappear once it has dried.

Santa Fairy-Light Night-light

This is a more time-consuming project to make. However, I really enjoyed making two of these night-lights for my boys, and they were so excited about having them in their rooms during the festive month! In this project, we will be using découpage to create Santa, his sack and presents. Not only does he look great during the day, but pop a string of fairy lights inside, and he glows magically throughout the night too!

You will need

* Washi tape or paint, to cover the jar lid

* Cardboard tube

* Wrapping paper scraps

* Strong glue

* PVA glue and water

* Soft paintbrush

* Red and white crepe paper

* Red, black and white glitter craft foam

* Brown packing paper

* White and pink/cream thin card

* Googly eyes

* Clear sellotape

* String

1 Cut a piece of white crepe paper to fit the dimensions of the jar sides. Cover the jar with a thin layer of PVA glue and water section by section, and press down the paper as you go. Gently paint another layer of PVA glue mix over the top, being careful not to rip the paper.

2 Cut out Santa's body. I have used a rough figure of eight shape for mine. The top of the shape is Santa's shoulders. Place the top of the shape two-thirds of the way up the jar. Paste over it with PVA mix.

5 Cut out an egg shape from pink/cream card for Santa's face. Paste it thoroughly to soften it before you stick it on, to one side of the neck of the sack. Paint over it with another layer of PVA mix.

3 To make the sack. Scrunch the brown packing paper repeatedly in your hands until it is slightly softened, with a wrinkled appearance. Now cut out the sack shape illustrated. The sack needs to fill the space from Santa's shoulders to the top of the jar, so you can measure this distance if you need to.

4 Paste the sack into place with PVA with the neck pointing downward and over Santa's left shoulder. Paste over the shape with more PVA mix.

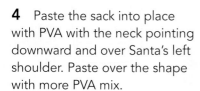

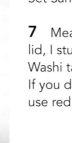

6 Cut a beard from white card and stick it to the lower half of Santa's face. Add a nose, googly eyes and a red smile. Set Santa aside to dry.

7 Meanwhile, to decorate the lid, I stuck a festively patterned Washi tape over the entire area. If you don't have Washi tape, use red or brown paint instead.

8 For the presents that sit on the lid (effectively in the sack), from cardboard form cubes and stick to hold in place.

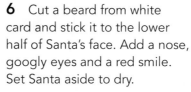

9 Wrap the mini presents in wrapping paper. Use small cuts of clear sticky tape to secure them. Embellish them with ribbon or small pom-poms, if you like.

10 Use strong glue to stick the presents securely to the top of the lid. The number you need will depend on the size of your jar.

11 Cut a Santa hat shape out of your red glitter craft foam. You will also need two boot shapes, two glove shapes, a belt and two buttons from your black foam. If you wish you can add a silver or gold buckle to your Santa belt too. You will then need to cut out white fur linings for your hat, gloves and boots. Stick the lining onto your shapes using strong glue. Allow to dry.

12 Once your jar is completely dry, you can stick the glitter foam shapes to it. Apply your strong glue to the back of all the shapes. Stick them to the jar, and as you go, cut lengths of string to tie around them, to hold the foam in shape while it dries. Your Santa should look a little 'tied up' when you're finished. Set aside to dry.

13 Cut off your string, pop in your fairy lights and screw on your lid. Make sure to twist the lid by holding the rim rather than the presents!

Festive Berries Floating Candle

These decorations are super quick to make, and visually stunning too. The beautiful bright hues of the berries and rich greens of the leaves contrast perfectly together, and the candle adds a romantic whimsy to the whole display. These are the perfect table decorations for long, dark winter afternoons, and festive evenings. They also look lovely sitting on a kitchen windowsill during the day.

It doesn't really matter what type of berries you use for this project. Stay clear of taking berries from public gardens, parks or highway displays, as these are usually protected by law.

Cut up your sprigs so that they fit in the jar, pop them in (gently, so you don't lose any berries) and top up with water.

If you have some twigs sticking up above the surface, trim them to fit. It is quite useful to place a couple of ends just under the surface, in the middle of the jar, to lightly rest your candle on.

Napkin Découpage

Last winter I was lucky enough to find a stack of traditional Christmas paper napkins. I used them to decorate these wonderful tea-light holders. There is no need to cut out any shapes or designs (unless you want to) as you can just paste them directly onto the jar as they are. Attaching a length of Christmas ribbon around the top adds a luxurious finishing touch.

From your mantelpiece to your windowsills, these napkin tea-lights will bring a glowing festive cheer to your home. They are such a simple way to add light and style to your Christmas décor.

1 Most paper serviettes have two or more layers of tissue paper in them. To achieve the best results, separate the top sheet with the design on it from the rest before you start. Save the rest of the sheets though, as you will be able to use them in future projects.

2 Use a mixture of PVA glue and water (about two parts glue to one part water) and a paintbrush. Paint the jar with the mixture before applying the tissue paper. Then gently paint a second layer of glue over the top.

3 If you'd like your jar to last a lifetime then paint a layer of clear matt or glass varnish over it to seal it.

Christmas Table Centrepiece

This is a grand centrepiece for a celebratory occasion. Perfect if you are having a large table for Christmas lunch!

This is a similar make to the Garden Chandelier project and uses the same method for preparing, cleaning and painting the chandelier, as well as selecting and securing your chosen jars. Please refer to that project to prepare your chandelier. The only thing you need to be aware of in this project is that your chandelier will have to sit level on your table, with the arms pointing upwards, to hold your jars.

You will need

* Silver spray paint

* Ivy, holly or similar evergreen

* Decorations such as small presents and red baubles

* Chandelier

* Strong glue

* Green garden wire

* Glue stick

1   Before you fix the jars to the chandelier, spray the insides of them with silver paint. Point your spray paint into the jar, and spray the base of it to give a lightly misted effect, which will allow candlelight to shine through.

2   Assemble the chandelier following the instructions for the Garden Chandelier project.

3   To add the decoration, generously wrap the ivy or other greenery around the base of each jar. Secure it with green garden wire. Now wrap it around the arms of the chandelier and up toward the top.

3   Using strong glue, stick on your decorations such as re-purposed jewellery, ribbon, small scale wrapped gifts, baubles, and stars. I have chosen some lovely little felt 'bauble' shapes.

Silhouette Snow Town

I adore this little make. The glow of the candle through the white snowy glitter creates a warm diffused light, which looks so pretty. A little patience is needed when you are cutting out the 'town', as some of the smaller details can be a little fiddly.

You will need

* White glitter

* Black glitter craft foam, or black card

* Glue stick

* Strong glue

* String

* Sharp craft knife

* Sticky tape

1 Wrap the glitter foam or card around the jar. Trim so that the ends overlap by 1 cm/½ in. Decide how high you would like your tallest tree or building to be, and trim the height of the card to size.

2 Protect the work surface with newspaper. Cover the jar in glue, applying it evenly with your glue stick. Leave a slither of clear glass at the base, where the lower strip of your town will be adhered. Gently shake glitter all over the jar. Once the jar is covered, set it aside to dry.

3 Turn the card or foam over and draw a town scene on the back beginning 2.5 cm/1 in up from the lower edge of the foam or card. Protecting the work surface, use a sharp craft knife to cut out the scene. Include lots of little windows.

4 If you are using card, use glue stick to cover the back of the card then stick it onto the jar.

5 If you are using craft foam, cover the back of the design with strong glue. Do not apply too much otherwise it will ooze out of the sides when you apply it to the jar. Wrap the foam around the jar and hold in place briefly with tape.

6 Cut a length of string and wrap it tightly around the base of the foam to hold it in place while it dries. You may also need to wrap string around the upper parts of the town, such as church spires, tall trees or lamp posts, to secure them while they adhere. Leave for 12 hours before removing the string.

7 Add either a candle or fairy lights into the jar.

Afterword

This is where I leave you. I hope you have enjoyed creating your fun and fabulous glass jar creations and that you, and your children, will cherish them for years to come. After writing this book, I now have a house full of re-purposed jars, homemade treats, fudge (ok, there's none of that left), gorgeous tea-light holders and a whole load of glitter. There will, no doubt, at some point in the future, be a battle of wills between my husband and myself, who will invariably try to cure my 'out of control' glass jar addiction. But for now, I am most definitely winning! And with the lovely projects in this book to encourage you, I hope you will be too!